A
STAR-SPANGLED
BIRTHDAY

The Delegates Leave Carpenter's Hall

H. A. Ogden

A
STAR-SPANGLED
BIRTHDAY

A Celebration in
Song, Poetry, Facts, and Trivia

GuildAmerica Books
Garden City, New York

Copyright © 2005 by Bookspan

Published by GuildAmerica Books, 501 Franklin Avenue, New York, New York 11530.

Edited by Elizabeth Mazer

Book design by Christos Peterson

ISBN: 1-58288-176-6

Printed in the United States of America

❧ Contents ❧

✥ Preface ✥

ON JULY 4, 1776, the representatives of the second Continental Congress took their final vote on a resolution written by Virginia delegate Thomas Jefferson, known as the Declaration of Independence. With that ordinary vote, made by those ordinary men, America made the extraordinary choice to declare itself free and independent from Great Britain. The day has gone down in more history books than can be counted, and the Declaration of Independence is commemorated across humankind every year, but the freedom that we celebrate had its roots before that day in 1776 and created a tradition that lasted long after.

To appreciate the value of the declaration passed on that historic day, the story has to begin with the spirit of revolution brewing in the colonies at that time that drove the colonists to seek freedom. And to truly value the impact that declaration has had since its passage, the story must continue from 1776 to today, to show the growth and celebration of the liberty we cherish. From the early days of the colonies' patriotic struggles to July 4, 1776, to all the Fourth of Julys that have followed, this volume shows, through poetry and prose, songs and speeches, and the magnificent Declaration of Independence itself, the struggle of our country from divided and dominated colonies to United States.

We have also included the biographies of the fifty-six men who signed the Declaration of Independence, showing their backgrounds as well as their involvement in the Revolutionary War, and the lives they led after the establishment of the United States. There's also a quiz packed with little-known facts about the Declaration of Independence and the men who signed it.

In final analysis, the Fourth of July is memorable not just because of the declaration that was passed, but because of the independence that document represented, and what it meant to the men who signed it and to the generations that followed. John Adams, member of the second Continental Congress and future president of the United States, described it best: "I am well aware," he wrote in a letter to his wife, Abigail, "of the Toil and Blood and Treasure, that it will cost Us to maintain this Declaration, and support and defend these States. Yet through all the Gloom I can see the Rays of ravishing Light and Glory. I can see that the End is more than worth all the Means. And that Posterity will tryumph in that Days Transaction."

A
STAR-SPANGLED
BIRTHDAY

❧ Yankee Doodle ❧

Early-American Traditional

Father and I went down to camp,
Along with Captain Gooding;
And there we saw the men and boys,
As thick as hasty pudding.

CHORUS
Yankee doodle, keep it up,
Yankee doodle dandy;
Mind the music and the step,
And with the girls be handy.

There was Captain Washington
Upon a slapping stallion,
A-giving orders to his men,
I guess there was a million.

CHORUS

And then the feathers on his hat,
They looked so' tarnal fin-a,
I wanted peskily to get
To give to my Jemima.

CHORUS

And then we saw a swamping gun,
Large as a log of maple;
Upon a deuced little cart,
A load for father's cattle.

CHORUS

And every time they shoot it off,
It takes a horn of powder;
It makes a noise like father's gun,
Only a nation louder.

CHORUS

I went as nigh to one myself,
As' Siah's underpinning;
And father went as nigh agin,
I thought the deuce was in him.

CHORUS

We saw a little barrel, too,
The heads were made of leather;
They knocked upon it with little clubs,
And called the folks together.

CHORUS

And there they'd fife away like fun,
And play on cornstalk fiddles,
And some had ribbons red as blood,
All bound around their middles.

CHORUS

The troopers, too, would gallop up
 And fire right in our faces;
 It scared me almost to death
 To see them run such races.

CHORUS

Uncle Sam came there to change
Some pancakes and some onions,
 For 'lasses cake to carry home
 To give his wife and young ones.

CHORUS

 But I can't tell half I see
 They kept up such a smother;
So I took my hat off, made a bow,
And scampered home to mother.

CHORUS

 Cousin Simon grew so bold,
I thought he would have cocked it;
 It scared me so I streaked it off,
 And hung by father's pocket.

CHORUS

And there I saw a pumpkin shell,
 As big as mother's basin;
And every time they touched it off,
 They scampered like the nation.

CHORUS

❧ Fourth of July Celebrations ❧

INDEPENDENCE DAY CELEBRATIONS began right away in 1776 along the Eastern Seaboard as soon as the colonies learned that the Declaration of Independence had been passed. On July 6, the *Pennsylvania Evening Post* was the first newspaper to print the declaration. Other papers in the colonies soon followed, leading to public readings and local celebrations spread across the newly proclaimed nation. One of the most notable took place in Williamsburg, Virginia, on July 25 with three readings of the Declaration of Independence, a military parade, and the firing of cannon and musketry. Meanwhile, in New York the declaration was read to the troops of the continental army, who celebrated by melting down the equestrian statue of George III for bullets.

The first organized festivities on July 4 took place in 1777 in Philadelphia, where the townspeople honored the first year of independence by firing cannons, one round for each state of the union; ringing bells, drinking toasts, and holding a parade, after which they set off fireworks. But in spite of the spirit of celebration, the status of the new nation was shaky at best. The Revolutionary War still raged on, and most celebrations, especially in battle zones, were relatively quiet, and often more spontaneous than planned. A classic example occurred in Mill Prison in 1778, where a group of American prisoners of war were only able to commemorate the Fourth of July by attaching homemade American flags to their hats.

The tide of the war had turned in favor of the colonists by 1781, and only months before Cornwallis's surrender to Washington at Yorktown, Virginia, Massachusetts passed the first legislative act for an official July 4 celebration. North Carolina followed suit in 1783 when Governor Alexander Martin issued a state order for celebration of the holiday. The other colonies soon formed their own laws and traditions, and the year 1804 provided another landmark when the first July 4 celebrations west of the Mississippi took place at Independence Creek, led by Meriwether Lewis and William Clark. Although July 4 wasn't declared an official federal holiday until 1941, by the mid-1800s Fourth of July celebrations were standard fare in most of the major cities in the United States.

Celebrations weren't limited to the United States. In the twentieth century, as our nation grew into an international power, July 4 festivities become worldwide events. One of the most striking examples occurred in the heart of World War I in 1917, when the citizens of Paris celebrated Independence Day as General John J. Pershing received American flags from French president Raymond Poincaré. By 1926, the 150th anniversary of the signing of the Declaration of Independence, the Fourth of July was honored from Budapest, Hungary, where Count Albert Apponyi gave a July 4 gratitude speech as church bells tolled, to London, England, where the *Morning Post*, the only major British paper dating back to 1776, printed a reproduction of the page from their August 17, 1776, issue with the full text of the Declaration of Independence. The first celebration headed by an American General Consulate, Paul Knabenshue, took place in Jerusalem in 1929 and set the tone for the many festivities to come around the globe in the following years. In 1992, July

4 celebrations went from international to intergalactic as the seven astronauts in the shuttle *Columbia* unfurled the American flag and chanted "Happy Birthday, America" from space.

While particular celebrations vary according to the location and the current state of the nation, the classic elements of an all-American July 4 party came into play early on. Even the Independence Day celebrations in the late 1700s included picnics, parades, and fireworks displays at night. In fact, fireworks and the firing of guns and cannons grew so dangerously popular that beginning in 1909 a nationwide movement was started to petition for a "safe and sane" July 4, hoping to cut down on the injuries occurring every year. As a result, ordinances were passed monitoring weapons and the sale and use of fireworks during the holiday. Today, most fireworks displays are handled by professionals, licensed by the city, and displayed under controlled conditions.

Through the years, however, the celebration of Independence Day has come to represent much more than picnics and parties. First and foremost, it is seen as a chance to remember and honor the events and the leaders who have shaped our country. In 1848, dignitaries from around the country gathered in Washington, D.C., to witness the laying of the cornerstone of the Washington Monument. On July 4, 1865, The National Monument Association went to Gettysburg to lay the cornerstone of the Soldier's Monument. Independence Day 1930 saw the carving of George Washington's face unveiled on Mount Rushmore in South Dakota. And in 1934, a plaque in memory of the Unknown Soldier was added to the permanent collection of memorial trophies at Arlington Cemetery.

To others, July 4 is seen as a call to arms. Independence Day reminds citizens of liberty fought for and won, and has led many Americans to stand up for their rights to further freedoms. The Civil Rights movement has strong ties to July 4, ranging from 1827, when New York emancipated its slaves on Independence Day, to 1837, when Oberlin students celebrated by holding antislavery meetings, to 1852 when Frederick Douglass presented his famous speech, "What to the Slave Is the Fourth of July." The connection extended past emancipation, exhibiting itself in 1961 when African Americans staged "swim-ins" at public swimming spots in Fort Lauderdale, Florida; and Lynchburg, Virginia; and later in 1991, when the National Civil Rights Museum was dedicated in Memphis, Tennessee.

Other movements have also found inspiration in the Fourth of July. The Women's Liberation movement has held countless demonstrations on Independence Day, most notably Susan B. Anthony's gathering in 1876 with other members of the National Woman's Suffrage Association to present and read their Declaration of Rights for Women at the Centennial Celebration. In 1887, *The New York Times* published an article calling for a new Declaration of Independence for commercial freedom in the world markets. President Emeritus of Harvard Charles W. Eliot called for a new Declaration of Independence "as a means of resisting the oppressive effects of industrial government" in 1911. And on July 4, 1925, the Women's Peace Union gathered in Battery Park in New York to present their Declaration of Independence from War.

For most of us, however, Independence Day is simply a chance to celebrate the American spirit. Independence Day has persevered through countless trials, ranging from its shaky beginning during the Revolutionary War, to darker days in the wars that have followed, to more recent times in our war against terror. Through all of it, Independence Day has remained as a beacon, reminding us what it is to have a country worth fighting for. In the most recent July 4 celebration in 2004, the cornerstone of the Freedom Tower was laid on the site of the World Trade Center in New York City, destroyed in the terrorist attacks of September 11, 2001. In his speech on this occasion, New York governor George E. Pataki reminded the world of the value of Independence Day.

> In signing the Declaration of Independence, our forefathers defiantly laid the cornerstone of our nation and unmistakably signaled its independence from foreign rule.
>
> Today, we, the heirs of that revolutionary spirit of defiance, lay this cornerstone and unmistakably signal to the world the unwavering strength of this nation, and our resolve to fight for freedom. . . .
>
> Let this great Freedom Tower show the world that what our enemies sought to destroy—our democracy, our freedom, our way of life—stands taller than ever.
>
> May God Bless the people of New York, and may God Bless the United States of America.

KEOKUK [IOWA]
❧ WEEKLY CONSTITUTION ❧
Wednesday, July 7, 1886
THE FOURTH.

How the Day was Celebrated in Keokuk Saturday.
A Large Display of Bunting All Over the City.
An Industrial Parade on Main Street in the Forenoon.
The Exercises at Rand Park in the Afternoon.
Good Music, Able Addresses and Orations.
A Pyrotechnic Display at Rand Park Closes the Day.

KEOKUK CELEBRATED THE Fourth of July this year on Saturday [July 3], and the occasion was taken advantage of by our home people. The day opened bright and clear, and continued so throughout the day, although the temperature was not as it generally is. Early in the day people began coming in from the neighborhood. Reception committee met the visitors on their arrival at the stations. The public buildings and business houses were decorated, as were quite a number of private residences. Red, white and blue bunting, bearing the inscription "1776 Welcome 1886" hung across Main street, at Fifth and Seventh, while the street was a mass of flags and bunting along the entire length. The day was

USHERED IN

By the ringing of bells and firing of a salute of thirteen guns at sunrise.

THE INDUSTRIAL PARADE

The industrial parade formed on Second and Main streets and a few minutes after 11 o'clock moved out Main to Fourteenth and thence back to Second under the direction of W. S. Sample, chief marshal, and Dr. J. C. Hughes, and Chas. F. Riffley, aides.

The procession was witnessed by several thousand of our people. The shoe department of the Enterprise was represented by the old woman who lived in the shoe, whose numerous progeny appeared from all sides of an enormous shoe. On Fred Dorr's float were a number of boys and girls eating ice cream.

A display of Japanese day fireworks at Sixth and Main streets wound up the programme for the morning.

AT RAND PARK

Several thousand people visited our beautiful Rand park during the day. The park was never so attractive as it is now, and the animals and birds have all comfortable quarters. Mark Twain was undoubtedly one of the attractions at the park, ranking well up with the bear. He was attired in an entire suite of white duck, with tall white hat, and on his appearance a murmur of "There he is," passed through the crowd, and people edged up to get a closer view of the great humorist.

The exercises at the grand stand at the park opened promptly at 2 o'clock with a selection by the Second Regiment band entitled "Robin Adair," with variations, and with cornet solo by Prof. Gus Wittich. Hon. Gibson Browne, president of the day, then called the meeting to order and prayer was offered by Rev. R. C. McIlwain, rector of St. John's Episcopal church. This was followed by music by the Second Regiment band—an overture, "Rivals"—followed by the reading of the Declaration of Independence by Orion Clemens, Esq. The Keokuk Military band then rendered an overture entitled "Brilliant," with saxophone solo by Prof. John Kindig.

Hon. Thomas Hedge, Jr., of Burlington, the orator of the day, was then introduced by Mr. Browne and spoke for thirty minutes, delivering one of the best addresses that has been given here on a pubic occasion. At the close he was heartily applauded.

Samuel L. Clemens was then introduced and his appearance was the signal for applause. His remarks were in substance as follows:

Ladies and gentlemen: I little thought that when the boys woke me with their noise this morning that I should be called upon to add to their noise. But I promise not to keep you long. You have heard all there is to hear on the subject, the evidence is all in and all I have to do is to sum up the evidence and deliver the verdict. You have heard the declaration of independence with its majestic ending, which is worthy to live forever, which has been hurled at the bones of a fossilized monarch, old King George the III, who has been dead these many years, and which will continue to be hurled at him annually as long as this republic lives. You have heard the history of the nation from the first to the last—from the beginning of the revolutionary war, past the days of its great general, Grant, told in eloquent language by the orator of the day. All I have to do is to add the verdict, which is all that can be added, and that is, "It is a successful day." I thank the officers of the day that I am enabled to once more stand face to face with the citizens that I met thirty years ago, when I was a citizen of Iowa, and also those of a later generation. In the address to-day, I have not heard much mention made of the progress of these last few years—of the telegraph, telephone, phonograph, and other great inventions. A poet has said, "Better fifty years of England than all the cycles of Cathay," but I say "Better this decade than the 900 years of Methuselah." There is more done in one year now than Methuselah ever saw in all his life. He was probably asleep all those 900 years. When I was here thirty years ago there were 3,000 people here and they drank 3,000 barrels of whisky a day, and they drank it in public then. I know that the man who makes the last speech on an occasion like this has the best of the other speakers, as he has the last word to say, which falls like a balm on the audience—though this audience has not been bored to-day—and though I can't say that last word, I will do the next best thing I can, and that is to sit down.

Mr. Clemens's remarks were frequently interrupted by laughter at his inimitable manner and the drollery of his utterance, and he closed amid laughter and applause.

The Keokuk Military band then gave a serenade, "Pleasant Dreams," after which the audience was dismissed with the benediction by Rev. T. H. Cleland, pastor of the First Westminster Presbyterian church.

THE AMUSEMENTS

At the conclusion of the exercise at the park, many people returned to Main street, where the climbing of the greased pole, wheelbarrow and sack races and lap race took place, and where some paper balloons were sent up.

The day's entertainment closed with a pyrotechnic display at Rand park at night, which was witnessed by a large concourse of people.

The Midnight Ride
of Paul Revere
by Henry Wadsworth Longfellow

Listen my children and you shall hear
Of the midnight ride of Paul Revere,
On the eighteenth of April, in Seventy-five;
Hardly a man is now alive
Who remembers that famous day and year.

He said to his friend, "If the British march
By land or sea from the town to-night,
Hang a lantern aloft in the belfry arch
Of the North Church tower as a signal light,—

One if by land, and two if by sea;
And I on the opposite shore will be,
Ready to ride and spread the alarm
Through every Middlesex village and farm,
For the country folk to be up and to arm."

Then he said "Good-night!" and with muffled oar
Silently rowed to the Charlestown shore,
Just as the moon rose over the bay,
Where swinging wide at her moorings lay
The Somerset, British man-of-war;
A phantom ship, with each mast and spar
Across the moon like a prison bar,

And a huge black hulk, that was magnified
By its own reflection in the tide.

Meanwhile, his friend through alley and street
Wanders and watches, with eager ears,
Till in the silence around him he hears
The muster of men at the barrack door,
The sound of arms, and the tramp of feet,
And the measured tread of the grenadiers,
Marching down to their boats on the shore.

Then he climbed the tower of the Old North Church,
By the wooden stairs, with stealthy tread,
To the belfry chamber overhead,
And startled the pigeons from their perch
On the sombre rafters, that round him made
Masses and moving shapes of shade,
By the trembling ladder, steep and tall,
To the highest window in the wall,
Where he paused to listen and look down
A moment on the roofs of the town
And the moonlight flowing over all.

Beneath, in the churchyard, lay the dead,
In their night encampment on the hill,
Wrapped in silence so deep and still
That he could hear, like a sentinel's tread,
The watchful night-wind, as it went
Creeping along from tent to tent,
And seeming to whisper, "All is well!"
A moment only he feels the spell
Of the place and the hour, and the secret dread
Of the lonely belfry and the dead;
For suddenly all his thoughts are bent

On a shadowy something far away,
Where the river widens to meet the bay,
A line of black that bends and floats
On the rising tide like a bridge of boats.

Meanwhile, impatient to mount and ride,
Booted and spurred, with a heavy stride
On the opposite shore walked Paul Revere.
Now he patted his horse's side,
Now he gazed at the landscape far and near,
Then, impetuous, stamped the earth,
And turned and tightened his saddle girth;
But mostly he watched with eager search
The belfry tower of the Old North Church,
As it rose above the graves on the hill,
Lonely and spectral and sombre and still.
And lo! as he looks, on the belfry's height
A glimmer, and then a gleam of light!
He springs to the saddle, the bridle he turns,
But lingers and gazes, till full on his sight
A second lamp in the belfry burns.

A hurry of hoofs in a village street,
A shape in the moonlight, a bulk in the dark,
And beneath, from the pebbles, in passing, a spark
Struck out by a steed flying fearless and fleet;
That was all! And yet, through the gloom and the light,
The fate of a nation was riding that night;
And the spark struck out by that steed, in his flight,
Kindled the land into flame with its heat.
He has left the village and mounted the steep,
And beneath him, tranquil and broad and deep,
Is the Mystic, meeting the ocean tides;
And under the alders that skirt its edge,

Now soft on the sand, now loud on the ledge,
Is heard the tramp of his steed as he rides.

It was twelve by the village clock
When he crossed the bridge into Medford town.
He heard the crowing of the cock,
And the barking of the farmer's dog,
And felt the damp of the river fog,
That rises after the sun goes down.

It was one by the village clock,
When he galloped into Lexington.
He saw the gilded weathercock
Swim in the moonlight as he passed,
And the meeting-house windows, black and bare,
Gaze at him with a spectral glare,
As if they already stood aghast
At the bloody work they would look upon.

It was two by the village clock,
When he came to the bridge in Concord town.
He heard the bleating of the flock,
And the twitter of birds among the trees,
And felt the breath of the morning breeze
Blowing over the meadow brown.
And one was safe and asleep in his bed
Who at the bridge would be first to fall,
Who that day would be lying dead,
Pierced by a British musket ball.

You know the rest. In the books you have read
How the British Regulars fired and fled,
How the farmers gave them ball for ball,
From behind each fence and farmyard wall,

Chasing the redcoats down the lane,
Then crossing the fields to emerge again
Under the trees at the turn of the road,
And only pausing to fire and load.

So through the night rode Paul Revere;
And so through the night went his cry of alarm
To every Middlesex village and farm,
A cry of defiance, and not of fear,
A voice in the darkness, a knock at the door,
And a word that shall echo for evermore!
For, borne on the night-wind of the Past,
Through all our history, to the last,
In the hour of darkness and peril and need,
The people will waken and listen to hear
The hurrying hoof-beats of that steed,
And the midnight message of Paul Revere.

Fourth of July Quiz

1. How many members of the Continental Congress signed the Declaration of Independence on July 4, 1776?

    A. 0
    B. 1
    C. 44
    D. 56

2. What was the "Committee of Five"?

    A. The delegates from Massachusetts.
    B. The congressional group that opposed the Declaration of Independence.
    C. The leadership of the Philadelphia branch of the Sons of Liberty.
    D. The committee appointed to write the Declaration of Independence.

3. What was the first "declaration" of independence from the Continental Congress?

    A. Lee's Resolution
    B. Otis's speech "In Opposition to Writs of Assistance"
    C. Articles of Confederation
    D. Declaration of Rights

4. How many colonies voted in favor of independence from Great Britain during the initial vote on July 1?

    A. 13
    B. 12
    C. 9
    D. 5

5. How old was Thomas Jefferson when he wrote the Declaration of Independence?

    A. 30
    B. 33
    C. 47
    D. 50

6. What was the range of ages of the signers of the Declaration of Independence?

    A. 25 years
    B. 35 years
    C. 45 years
    D. 55 years

7. Who is the only known signer of the Association of 1774, the Declaration of Independence, the Articles of Confederation, and the U.S. Constitution?

    A. Benjamin Franklin
    B. George Washington
    C. Roger Sherman
    D. George Clymer

8. What was the first meeting place of the Continental Congress?

A. Carpenter's Hall
B. Independence Hall
C. Pennsylvania State House
D. Old City Hall

9. How many signers were born outside the colonies?

A. 5
B. 8
C. 11
D. 14

10. Who was the first signer of the Declaration of Independence to die?

A. John Morton
B. Philip Livingston
C. Benjamin Franklin
D. George Ross

11. Who was the last signer of the Declaration of Independence to die?

A. William Floyd
B. William Ellery
C. John Adams
D. Charles Carroll

12. Which signer of the Declaration of Independence has no known date of death?

A. James Smith
B. Thomas Lynch Jr.
C. Button Gwinnett
D. John Hart

13. Who was the last man to sign the Declaration of Independence?

A. Oliver Wolcott
B. George Wythe
C. Thomas McKean
D. Matthew Thornton

14. Of the charges against King George III that Thomas Jefferson initially included in the Declaration of Independence, which charge was dropped by the final version?

A. Taxation without representation
B. Promoting the slave trade
C. Waging war against the colonies
D. Impressments of sailors

15. Which signer of the Declaration of Independence is credited with designing the U.S. flag?

A. Francis Hopkinson
B. Joseph Hewes
C. Carter Braxton
D. Robert Morris

16. How many signers of the Declaration of Independence were not members of the Continental Congress on July 4, 1776?

A. 13
B. 10
C. 6
D. 4

17. Which pair of brothers signed the Declaration of Independence?

A. John Adams and Samuel Adams
B. Edward Rutledge and John Rutledge
C. Philip Livingston and William Livingston
D. Francis Lightfoot Lee and Richard Henry Lee

18. Of the first five presidents of the United States, how many signed the Declaration of Independence?

A. 4
B. 3
C. 2
D. 1

19. Which two signers were the ancestors of presidents?

A. James Wilson and Josiah Bartlett
B. John Adams and Benjamin Harrison
C. Benjamin Harrison and James Wilson
D. John Adams and James Wilson

20. Which two signers died on the fiftieth anniversary of the signing of the Declaration of Independence?

    A. John Adams and Thomas Jefferson
    B. James Madison and James Smith
    C. Stephen Hopkins and George Ross
    D. Roger Sherman and Elbridge Gerry

Answers

1. B   Only one person signed the Declaration of Independence on July 4. When Congress adjourned that afternoon after having voted to adopt the Declaration of Independence, John Hancock, president of the Congress, was charged with authenticating the revised document, signing it, and sending copies to the colonial legislatures and the army for approval. The first printed copies bore only the names of Hancock and Charles Thomson, who was not a signer but whose name appeared on the documents due to his position as secretary of the Congress. The rest of the delegates did not sign until August 2 or later.

2. D   The "Committee of Five" consisted of John Adams of Massachusetts, Roger Sherman of Connecticut, Benjamin Franklin of Pennsylvania, Robert R. Livingston of New York, and Thomas Jefferson of Virginia, who were charged with writing the Declaration of Independence. The committee voted to turn the task over to Thomas Jefferson, believing him to be the most eloquent writer, but he consulted with John Adams and Benjamin Franklin for corrections before submitting it to Congress. It's unknown how much help Sherman and Livingston were, especially since Livingston refused to sign the Declaration of Independence once it was passed, thinking the Congress was acting too quickly.

3. A   Lee's Resolution, presented to the Continental Congress on June 7, 1776, by delegate Richard Henry Lee of Virginia, was the first declaration of intent to separate from Great Britain as follows:

"Resolved: That these United Colonies are, and of right ought to be, free and independent States, that they are absolved from all allegiance to the British Crown, and that all political connection between them and the State of Great Britain is, and ought to be, totally dissolved." Congress voted on a three-week recess to consider the matter, during which they selected the Committee of Five to draft a declaration in line with Lee's resolution. The result was the Declaration of Independence.

4. C   Nine colonies initially voted in favor of independence; Pennsylvania and South Carolina voted against it while Delaware was undecided and New York, having expected authorization from home, which they did not receive, abstained. South Carolina gave in the next day for the sake of unanimity. Pennsylvania changed its vote when two of the delegates stayed home, meaning that the majority of the delegates were in its favor. Caesar Rodney, an absent delegate from Delaware, was summoned and rode for eighty miles to get there in time to break the tie from his state. Since New York expected any day to receive authorization, the Congress was able to pass the measure with a unanimous vote. New York actually received authorization on July 19, which was when the declaration was authorized to be printed for signing.

5. B   Thomas Jefferson was thirty-three when he wrote the Declaration of Independence.

6. C   There was a range of forty-five years: the youngest signer, Edward Rutledge of South Carolina, was twenty-six while the oldest signer, Benjamin Franklin, was seventy.

7. C   Roger Sherman of Connecticut.

8. A   Carpenter's Hall was the meeting place of the first Continental Congress. They moved to the Pennsylvania State House, now known as Independence Hall, in spring 1775 to have more room.

9. B   Eight signers were born outside the colonies: Button Gwinnett (England), Francis Lewis (Wales), Robert Morris (England), James Smith (Ireland), George Taylor (Ireland), Matthew Thornton (Ireland), James Wilson (Scotland), and John Witherspoon (Scotland).

10. A In April 1777, John Morton became the first signer of the Declaration of Independence to die.

11. D Charles Carroll outlived all his fellow signers, dying November 14, 1832.

12. B Thomas Lynch Jr. vanished at sea in late 1776 on a boat headed to the West Indies. Neither the boat nor his body were ever recovered.

13. C Thomas McKean was the last person to sign the Declaration of Independence. Although he was present for the July 4 vote, he left the Congress to serve in the militia and wasn't there in August when the document returned from the printers. It's unknown exactly when he signed the declaration, but his name was not on the authenticated copy sent by Congress to the states on January 18, 1777. It is supposed that he signed it later.

14. B The declaration initially condemned King George for promoting the "execrable commerce determining to keep open a market where MEN should be bought and sold." Although a slaveholder himself, Jefferson was strongly against slavery as an institution. His fellow slaveholders in Congress disagreed, and fought against including that offense in the Declaration of Independence. For the sake of unanimity, the passage was dropped.

15. A Francis Hopkinson was chairman of the Navy Board from 1776 to 1778. In that post, he may have been responsible for designing the first official national flag, known as the Stars and Stripes, which was approved by the Continental Congress on June 14, 1777.

16. C Six signers of the Declaration of Independence joined the Continental Congress after July 4: Matthew Thornton, Benjamin Rush, George Clymer, James Wilson, George Ross, and George Taylor.

17. D Brothers Francis Lightfoot Lee and Richard Henry Lee of Virginia were co-signers of the Declaration of Independence.

18. C Just two of the first five presidents signed the Declaration of Independence: the second president, John Adams, and the third president, Thomas Jefferson. George Washington was a member of the Continental Congress in the summer of 1776, but he was off leading the continental army and was not available to sign the declaration. The fourth president, James Madison, didn't join the Continental Congress until 1780 while the fifth president, James Monroe, joined the Congress in 1783.

19. B The sixth president, John Quincy Adams, was the son of signer John Adams. William Henry Harrison, son of Benjamin Harrison, was the ninth president while his grandson, also named Benjamin Harrison, served as the twenty-third president.

20. A Thomas Jefferson and John Adams both died on July 4, 1826, within hours of each other.

America the Beautiful
by Katharine Lee Bates

O beautiful for spacious skies,
For amber waves of grain,
For purple mountain majesties
Above the fruited plain!
America! America!
God shed His grace on thee
And crown thy good with brotherhood
From sea to shining sea!

O beautiful for pilgrim feet,
Whose stern, impassion'd stress
A thoroughfare for freedom beat
Across the wilderness!
America! America!
God mend thine ev'ry flaw,
Confirm thy soul in self-control,
Thy liberty in law!

O beautiful for heroes proved
In liberating strife,
Who more than self their country loved,
And mercy more than life!
America! America!
May God thy gold refine,
Till all success be nobleness,
And ev'ry gain divine!

O beautiful for patriot dream
That sees beyond the years
Thine alabaster cities gleam,
Undimm'd by human tears!
America! America!
God shed His grace on thee
And crown thy good with brotherhood
From sea to shining sea!

❧ "Give Me Liberty or Give Me Death" ❧
by Patrick Henry
March 23, 1775

MR. PRESIDENT: IT is natural to man to indulge in the illusions of hope. We are apt to shut our eyes against a painful truth— and listen to the song of that siren, till she transforms us into beasts. Is this the part of wise men, engaged in a great and arduous struggle for liberty? Are we disposed to be of the number of those, who having eyes, see not, and having ears, hear not, the things which so nearly concern their temporal salvation? For my part, whatever anguish of spirit it may cost, I am willing to know the whole truth; to know the worst, and to provide for it.

I have but one lamp by which my feet are guided; and that is the lamp of experience. I know of no way of judging of the future but by the past. And judging by the past, I wish to know what there has been in the conduct of the British ministry for the last ten years, to justify those hopes with which gentlemen have been pleased to solace themselves and the house? Is it that insidious smile with which our petition has been lately received? Trust it not, sir; it will prove a snare to your feet. Suffer not yourselves to be betrayed with a kiss. Ask yourselves how this gracious reception of our petition comports with those warlike preparations which cover our waters and darken our land. Are fleets and armies necessary to a work of love and reconciliation? Have we shown our-selves so unwilling to be reconciled that force must be called in to win back our love? Let us not deceive ourselves, sir. These are the implements of war and subjugation—the last arguments to which kings resort. I ask gentlemen, sir, what means this martial array, if its purpose be not to force us to submission? Can gentlemen assign any other possible motive for it? Has Great Britain any enemy in this quarter of the world, to call for all this accumulation of navies and armies? No, sir, she has none. They are meant for us: they can be meant for no other. They are sent over to bind and rivet upon us those chains which the British ministry have been so long forging. And what have we to oppose to them? Shall we try argument? Sir, we have been trying that for the last ten years. Have we anything new to offer upon the subject? Nothing. We have held the subject up in every light of which it is capable; but it has been all in vain. Shall we resort to entreaty and humble supplication? What terms shall we find which have not been already exhausted? Let us not, I beseech you, sir, deceive ourselves longer.

Sir, we have done everything that could be done to avert the storm which is now coming on. We have petitioned—we have remonstrated—we have supplicated—we have prostrated ourselves before the throne, and have implored its interposition to arrest the tyrannical hands of the ministry and parliament. Our petitions have been slighted; our remonstrances have produced additional violence and insult; our supplications have been disregarded; and we have been spurned, with contempt, from the foot of the throne. In vain, after these things, may we indulge the fond hope of peace and reconciliation. There is no longer any room for hope. If we wish to be free—if we mean to preserve inviolate those inestimable privileges for which we have been so long contending—if we mean not basely to abandon the noble struggle in which we have been so long engaged, and which we have pledged ourselves never to abandon until the glorious object of our contest shall be obtained—we must fight!—I repeat it, sir, we must fight! An appeal to arms and to the God of Hosts, is all that is left us!

They tell us, sir, that we are weak—unable to cope with so formidable an adversary. But when shall we be stronger? Will it be the next week or the next year? Will it be when we are totally disarmed, and when a British guard shall be stationed in every house? Shall we gather strength by irresolution and inaction? Shall we acquire the means of effectual resistance by lying supinely on our backs, and hugging the delusive phantom of hope, until our enemies shall have bound us hand and foot? Sir, we are not weak, if we make a proper use of those means which the God of nature has placed in our power. Three millions of people, armed in the holy cause of liberty, and in such a country as that which we possess, are invincible by any force which our enemy can send against us. Besides, sir, we shall not fight our battles alone. There is a just God who presides over the destinies of nations; and who will raise up friends to fight our battles for us. The battle, sir, is not to the strong alone; it is to the vigilant, the active, the brave. Besides, sir, we have no election. If we were base enough to desire it, it is now too late to retire from the contest. There is no retreat but in submission and slavery! Our chains are forged. Their clanking may be heard on the plains of Boston! The war is inevitable and let it come! I repeat it, sir, let it come!

It is in vain, sir, to extenuate the matter. Gentlemen may cry, peace, peace—but there is no peace. The war is actually begun! The next gale that sweeps from the north will bring to our ears the clash of resounding arms! Our brethren are already in the field! Why stand we here idle? What is it that gentlemen wish? What would they have? Is life so dear, or peace so sweet, as to be purchased at the price of chains and slavery? Forbid it, Almighty God!—I know not what course others may take; but as for me, give me liberty or give me death!

The Signers of the
∾ Declaration of Independence ∾

MASSACHUSETTS

John Hancock was born in Braintree, Massachusetts, on January 12, 1737, to a clergyman who died when he was still a child. He was adopted by his father's brother Thomas, one of the wealthiest merchants in New England. Hancock attended Harvard and received his degree in 1754, after which he worked as a clerk in his uncle's counting house. He spent some time in England on business and witnessed the coronation of George III, but returned to America after his uncle's death in 1763 to take over the counting house. When the British taxes began interfering with business, he grew involved in politics, building friendships with many of Boston's leading politicians, such as James Otis, Thomas Cushing, and Samuel Adams. In October 1774, Hancock was elected to the Continental Congress and took on the role of president in 1775 when Peyton Randolph resigned. It was in this post that his signature headed the Declaration of Independence. Hancock retired from the Continental Congress in October 1777, but was named the first governor of Massachusetts in 1780, an office that he held nine times before his death on October 8, 1793.

Samuel Adams was born in Boston, Massachusetts, on September 22, 1722. Adams began his studies at Harvard in 1736, working his way through as a waiter in the college dining hall after his father lost most of the family's money in a bad business deal during Adams's junior year. He graduated with his masters in 1743 and became a clerk in the counting house of Thomas Cushing. After failing spectacularly in business and losing all the capital his father had given him, Adams turned to politics. In 1765, he was elected as a representative to the general court of Massachusetts, where he quickly attracted notice. Less publicly, he helped form the secret organization the Sons of Liberty to oppose the British with acts like the Boston Tea Party on December 16, 1773. Adams was a member of the first Continental Congress that assembled in Philadelphia on September 5, 1774, and continued to serve there until 1781. In 1789, he was elected lieutenant governor of Massachusetts and held that office till 1794, when he was chosen as governor, a position he kept until his retirement in 1797. He died on October 2, 1803.

John Adams was born in Braintree, Massachusetts, on October 19, 1735. He graduated from Harvard in 1755 and was admitted to the bar six years later. He joined the Continental Congress in 1774, where he was so well known for favoring independence that he was placed on the committee to draft the Declaration of Independence. In 1778, he went to France to rally support for the Revolutionary War, and established himself as a diplomat. Adams orchestrated the peace treaty with Britain so ably that in 1785 he began serving as envoy to the British court. Returning to America in 1788 to serve as vice president under George Washington, he was elected president in 1796 and was the first president to live in the White House. Difficulties in France, along with political skirmishes in America, reduced his popularity and he lost re-election to Jefferson, after which he retired to Quincy, Massachusetts. He lived long enough to see his son, John Quincy Adams, inaugurated as the sixth president in 1825, but died a year later, on July 4, 1826, exactly fifty years after the signing of the Declaration of Independence. His last words were "Thomas Jefferson survives," unaware that Jefferson himself had died mere hours before.

Robert Treat Paine was a native of Boston, born on March 11, 1731. He served as a chaplain during the French and Indian War, but gave it up after a few years to pursue the study of law. Once he was admitted to the bar, Paine settled into practice in Taunton, where he lived for many years. In 1770, he conducted the prosecution for the soldiers indicted for the Boston Massacre and from this time he began to take a more active role in politics, particularly when he was elected as a representative to the general assembly. In 1774, he became a member of the Continental Congress. He was reelected as delegate in 1775 and 1776, and voted with the others for the Declaration of Independence even though he authored the final appeal to the king in 1775, known as the Olive Branch Petition. Paine continued as a member of the Continental Congress until 1777 when he was appointed the first attorney general of Massachusetts. He held the post until 1780, when he was transferred to a seat on the Massachusetts Supreme Court. There he remained until his retirement in 1804. He died on May 11, 1814.

Elbridge Gerry was born in Marblehead, Massachusetts, on July 17, 1744. Gerry attended Harvard with the intention of studying medicine, but chose instead to join his father's mercantile business after school. He did well in business and soon built a strong reputation in Marblehead. In May 1772, he was appointed to the general court and in February 1775 he joined a provincial Congress that worked to build defenses against the British by arming the militia. When the British planned a raid on the militia's stores in Concord and Lexington, Gerry barely managed to escape a detachment of soldiers by hiding in his nightclothes in a cornfield in the middle of the night. The soldiers continued onward, sparking the legendary battles of Lexington and Concord. On February 9, 1776, Gerry was elected to the Continental Congress where he signed the Declaration of Independence, and helped draw up the Articles of Confederation. He served two terms in the U.S. Congress before 1797, when he was appointed ambassador to France. He returned to America in 1798 and served two terms as governor of Massachusetts. In 1812, he was elected vice president under James Madison. He died in office on November 23, 1814.

NEW HAMPSHIRE

Josiah Bartlett was born in Amesbury, Massachusetts, on November 21, 1729. When he was sixteen, he began to study medicine under Dr. Ordway of Amesbury. He moved to Kingston, New Hampshire, in 1750, where he opened his own practice. In 1765, Bartlett was elected to the New Hampshire legislature, where he was outspoken in his opposition to the royal governor, John Wentworth, even after Wentworth appointed Bartlett justice of the peace. In September 1775, Bartlett took his seat in the Continental Congress. When the vote was called for the Declaration of Independence, the names were called beginning with the northernmost colony, meaning that Bartlett was the first to vote in its favor. In 1779, he became the chief justice of the New Hampshire court of common pleas, from which he advanced to associate justice and then chief justice of the superior court. He was elected president of New Hampshire for three years. When the title changed to governor in 1793, he was the first to win it. During his administration, in the year 1791, he chartered the New Hampshire Medical Society and served as their first president. He retired from public office in 1794 and died on May 19, 1795.

William Whipple was born in Kittery, Maine, on January 14, 1730. After finishing school, Whipple went off to sea aboard a merchant vessel to gain his fortune. Following a string of successes, he settled into Portsmouth in 1759 and soon established himself in business with his brother. After prominent local service in Portsmouth, he was appointed to the second Continental Congress in 1776. His service to Congress continued until 1779 and was interrupted only by his military service when he commanded the New Hampshire troops as brigadier general in the Saratoga campaign. After leaving Congress, he was elected to his state legislature and from 1782 until his death in 1785 he served as an associate justice of the superior court. He died on November 28, 1785.

Matthew Thornton was born in Ireland in 1714. He immigrated to Wiscasset, Maine, when he was about four years old and moved a few years later to Worcester, Massachusetts. He studied medicine under Dr. Grout of Leicester, after which he opened his own practice in Londonberry, New Hampshire. He served as an "under-surgeon" to the New Hampshire troops during the Louisburg expedition of 1746 and eventually, in later years, rose to the rank of colonel in the militia. In 1775, the royal governor of New Hampshire fled to avoid the rising protests, and a provincial convention was established to govern in his place. Thornton served as its president and drafted a constitution for the state. He was elected to the Continental Congress in 1776, but did not take his seat until November 4. Like his fellow New Hampshire delegates, Thornton became a member of the judiciary of New Hampshire, serving as an associate justice of the superior court for many years. He died in Newburyport, Massachusetts, during a visit to his daughter, on June 24, 1803.

RHODE ISLAND

Stephen Hopkins was born on March 7, 1707, in Cranston, Rhode Island. While he made his living as a merchant, he first held public office at the age of twenty-five, and continued to do so almost without break for the rest of his life. Hopkins served as assistant justice of the superior court in the years 1747–49; from 1751 to 1755 he was chief justice of this court. He was an early and energetic defender of colonial rights, and in 1772, when the British revenue cutter *The Gaspee* was burned by a group of prominent Providence citizens in a gesture of defiance against the British regulations, Hopkins refused, in his post as chief justice, to allow the participants to be prosecuted. Hopkins served as a Rhode Island delegate to the first two sessions of the Continental Congress. Although he left the Congress in September 1776 due to failing health, he continued to perform local public service for many years, including serving as first chancellor of Rhode Island College, now known as Brown University. He died on July 13, 1785.

William Ellery was born in Newport, Rhode Island, on December 22, 1727. His early education was handled exclusively by his father, a Harvard graduate, who prepared his son to enter his alma mater at the age of sixteen. After his graduation, Ellery returned to Newport where he studied law and soon opened his own practice. He was elected to the Continental Congress in 1776 and is said to have reported that at the signing of the Declaration of Independence the faces of each of the delegates as they affixed their names showed "undaunted resolution." He served as an active member of the Congress, for all but two years, from 1776 to 1786 and was particularly noted for his committee work on commercial and naval affairs. In 1790, President George Washington appointed him collector of customs for the Newport district. He held this post until his death on February 15, 1820.

CONNECTICUT

Roger Sherman was born in Newton, Massachusetts, on April 19, 1721. His family could not afford to give him a prestigious education, so they apprenticed him to a shoemaker, where he worked until he was twenty-two. In 1743, he moved to New Milford, Connecticut, where he soon entered into a mercantile partnership with his brother. Sherman believed in self-education and in 1754 his studies resulted in his admittance to the bar. He quickly became popular as a local official, both in New Milford and in New Haven, where he moved in 1761. He was known for the number of offices he held concurrently, including his office as treasurer of Yale College, which gave him an a honorary M.A. degree. He was, with the interruption of only one year, a member of the Continental Congress from the first session in 1774 through 1784, after which he served as a member of the Constitutional Convention of 1787 and was responsible for the Great Compromise of the Constitution. From 1784 until his death, he was mayor of New Haven. He also served as a

U.S. representative in 1789–91 and as a U.S. senator from 1791 until his death on July 23, 1793.

Oliver Wolcott was born to the colonial governor in Windsor, Connecticut, on December 1, 1726. He graduated from Yale in 1747 at the top of his class and was immediately commissioned by the royal governor of New York, George Clinton, to raise a volunteer militia that he led as captain in the French and Indian War. Following the war he settled in Litchfield, where he was the sheriff for more than twenty years and served as a member of the general assembly from 1771 to 1786. He was elected to the Continental Congress in 1775, but had to leave in June of 1776 because of illness and was not present for the voting on the Declaration of Independence. He signed it on his return to Philadelphia in October. Afterwards, he returned almost immediately to Connecticut, where he became engaged in military affairs, serving as a general in the Saratoga campaign, though he continued to serve as delegate to the Continental Congress until 1778 and then again from 1780 to 1784. He won the office of lieutenant governor of Connecticut in 1786 and continued to serve until he was elected governor in 1796, a position he held until his death on December 1, 1797.

William Williams was born in Lebanon, Connecticut, on April 8, 1731. He entered Harvard at age sixteen and following his graduation in 1751 he studied theology with his father, who was pastor of the First Congregational Church in Lebanon. In September 1755, he fought in the French and Indian War at Lake George, New York, after which he returned to Lebanon and established himself as a merchant. He also took a job as town clerk, which he held for forty-four years, and served many years as a selectman and a member of the lower house of legislature. He resigned a colonel's commission in order to join the

Continental Congress in the summer of 1776, taking the place of Oliver Wolcott. During his period of office, he signed the Declaration of Independence and was appointed a member of the committee to frame the Articles of Confederation. He served as a delegate to the state convention of 1788, where he voted for the ratification of the U.S. Constitution. Afterwards, he retired to Lebanon to serve as a county court judge. He died on August 2, 1811.

Samuel Huntington was born the eldest son of a poor farmer in Windham, Connecticut, on July 2, 1732. Though he received very little formal schooling, he studied law on his own and gained admittance to the bar at the age of twenty-three. He opened his first practice in Windham, but moved to Norwich in 1760, where he was appointed king's attorney for the region. In 1773, he became an associate judge in the superior court and soon after an assistant in the council of Connecticut. It was also in this period that he began his association with the local branch of the Sons of Liberty. He was elected to the Continental Congress of 1775–81, serving as president from 1779 to 1781. Poor health required him to return to Connecticut, where the offices of judge in the superior court and assistant in the council had both been kept vacant in his absence. In 1783, he served another term in the Continental Congress, after which he returned to Connecticut to serve as lieutenant governor until 1786, when he was elected governor. He continued to hold that office until his death on January 5, 1796.

NEW YORK

Francis Lewis was the only signer of the Declaration of Independence from Wales. He was born in Llandaff, South

Wales, in March 1713. After the death of his parents, Lewis was raised by an aunt who sent him to Scotland to be educated. He completed his education in Westminster, after which he began working in the counting room of a London merchant. When he was in his early twenties, he collected the property left to him by his father, traded it for merchandise, and sailed for New York. During the French and Indian War, Lewis was a supply agent for the British troops and was rewarded for his services with a grant for five thousand acres of land. Despite his association with the British government, he quickly took to the patriotic cause, becoming a member of the Sons of Liberty. He was elected to the Continental Congress in 1775 and remained a member until 1779. His patriotism cost him dearly when his home was ransacked and burned by the British, with his wife taken prisoner, during the course of the war. He lost most of his fortune and died in comparative poverty on December 31, 1802.

Philip Livingston was born in Albany, New York, on January 15, 1716. He graduated from Yale College in 1737 and began his mercantile career in New York City. He donated generously to a number of public causes and was one of the earliest advocates of King's College, now known as Columbia University, as well as one of the moving forces behind the organization of the New York Society Library. He was elected alderman in 1754 and continued his public service in that office, as well as in the provincial assembly, where he served as Speaker. He was elected to the Continental Congress in 1774 and continued as a member through 1777, signing the Declaration of Independence with the others in August even though his absences during June and July 1776 prevented him from placing his vote. Livingston was elected to the New York state senate in 1777, where he served for one year, after which he became a U.S. representative. He died in office on June 12, 1778.

Lewis Morris was born in Morrisania, New York, now known as the Bronx, on April 8, 1726. Morris, who came from a wealthy family, began his education at Yale at the age of sixteen and received his degree in 1746. After his father's death, he took part in some local politics, serving as a member of the provincial legislature before it was dissolved by the British. He was selected as a New York delegate to the second Continental Congress, where he served from 1775 to 1777. In June 1776, he left Congress to lead the Westchester militia and missed the July 4 vote. He was, however, a member of the provincial Congress of New York that approved the declaration, and he signed it when he returned to Philadelphia in September. His fortune was hard hit by the Revolutionary War, and he spent most of his time after the war working to restore it. He served for a while as a judge in Worchester and as a member of the upper house of the new legislature. He continued to be prominent in local affairs and was on the first Board of Regents for the University of New York. He died on January 22, 1798.

William Floyd was born on Long Island, New York, on December 17, 1734, the son of a wealthy landholder. When he was a teenager, Floyd was forced by his father's death to curtail his education in order to run the family's large estate. He became involved in political struggles early on and rose to the rank of major general in the Suffolk County militia. He served in the first and the second Continental Congresses, where he focused his efforts on the admiralty and the treasury committees. While attending Congress in Philadelphia, the British army took possession of Long Island, destroying

Floyd's estate and forcing his family to take refuge in Connecticut, where they remained for the rest of the war. He was a state senator from 1784 to 1788, and a U.S. representative from 1789 to 1791. He then returned to New York, where he bought land along the Mohawk River, developing it into a farm that he made his primary residence in 1803. In 1808, he was elected to serve one last term as a New York state senator, after which he retired from politics and devoted the rest of his life to farming. He died on August 4, 1821.

NEW JERSEY

John Hart was born in Stonington, Connecticut, in 1711. His education was minimal, but he ran his farm and mills very successfully and was a respected member of the community. He began his career in public office as a member of the New Jersey provincial assembly, where he served from 1761 until the assembly was dissolved in 1771. Hart also served as a judge in the Hunterdon County courts from 1768 to 1775. He was elected a member of the Continental Congress on June 22, 1776. In November 1776, New Jersey was overrun by the British, and Hart's lands and mills were laid to waste. In spite of the danger, he continued to support the revolution, serving as Speaker on the first state general assembly under the state Constitution in August 1776. In 1778, when battle brought troops from the continental army near Hart's land in Hopewell, he invited them to encamp on his farm. George Washington lunched with Hart, after which Washington held his famous Council of War at the nearby Hunt House. Twelve thousand men camped on Hart's fields for two days—during the growing season. Hart died on his estate less than a year later, on May 11, 1779.

John Witherspoon was born near Edinburgh, Scotland, on February 15, 1723. He studied at the University of Edinburgh and then attended divinity school. After establishing himself in a parish and earning his doctorate, he was approached by Richard Stockton and Benjamin Rush, who invited him to serve as the first president of the College of New Jersey, now known as Princeton University. Witherspoon arrived in America in August 1768 and devoted the next six years to reforming the school. He was elected to the Continental Congress in 1776, where he was firmly and fervently in favor of American independence, saying during a speech on July 2 that America was "not only ripe for the measure but in danger of rotting for the want of it." He continued to serve in the Congress almost continuously until 1782, after which he returned to New Jersey. The campus of his college had been practically destroyed by the British, and Witherspoon dedicated most of his time to rebuilding it, participating in local politics, and promoting the growth of the Presbyterian Church. He died on November 15, 1794.

Richard Stockton was born near Princeton, New Jersey, on October 1, 1730. He was educated at the West Nottingham Academy and received his degree from the College of New Jersey in 1748. He studied law with David Ogden of Newark, and soon became a prominent lawyer, with one of the largest practices in the colonies. He maintained close ties to the College of New Jersey and traveled to Scotland in 1767 to convince John Witherspoon to serve as the college's first president. Initially, he was a political moderate, hoping to reconcile with Britain, but as relations grew increasingly hostile he came to see independence as the only solution. In 1776, when word reached New Jersey that their delegates to Congress were holding out against independence, Stockton and Witherspoon were sent to replace other New Jersey representatives, with instructions to vote for independence. That November, Stockton returned from an inspection of the northern army to find his state overrun by the British. He was able to get his family to safety, but was unable to avoid capture himself. Congress negotiated his exchange, but the captivity ruined his health as well as his finances. He died a pauper on February 28, 1781.

Abraham Clark was born in Elizabethtown, New Jersey, on February 15, 1726, the only son of a farmer. Too frail to work the farm with his father, he began his career in surveying. He studied law on the side and, while he was never officially admitted to the bar, he was known for the legal advice he gave, earning him the title "the poor man's counselor." He was well known for his criticism on the pretensions of lawyers, which won him some enemies among the educated elite but earned him a large share of popular approval. He was elected sheriff for Essex County and then to the provincial Congress in 1775. From there, he was sent to represent New Jersey in the second Continental Congress. He remained in Congress for several years, serving terms in the New Jersey legislature in the interims. Though illness prevented him from attending the Constitutional Convention of 1787, he remained active in politics, serving in the second and third sessions of the U.S. Congress under the new Constitution. He retired after the adjournment of Congress in June 1794 and died shortly after on September 15, 1794.

Francis Hopkinson was born in Philadelphia on September 21, 1737, the son of Thomas Hopkinson, a prominent lawyer and one of the founders of the American Philosophical Society. Hopkinson attended the College of Philadelphia, later affiliated with the University of Pennsylvania, where he studied law. He finished his education in England, studying under the Bishop of Worcester. After two years away, he returned to America and began building his law practice. Versatile and engaging, Hopkinson was an accomplished poet, essayist, and musician, and a skillful satirist. He married Ann Borden, who was from a prominent New Jersey family, and moved with her to Bordentown, New Jersey, where he became politically active. In his satirical pieces against the British, he made his views on the necessity of independence very clear. Hopkinson was elected to the Continental Congress in 1776, after which he became chairman of the Navy Board. In this role, he is thought to have designed the first American flag. Beginning in 1779, he served as judge of admiralty for Pennsylvania. George Washington appointed him Federal District Judge for Pennsylvania in 1789, and he held the post until his death on May 9, 1791.

PENNSYLVANIA

Benjamin Franklin was born in Boston on January 17, 1706. His father apprenticed him to his brother James, printer of *The New-England Courant*, where Franklin published his first article anonymously in 1721. He settled in Philadelphia, setting up his own printing shop in 1732. In 1741 he began *Poor Richard's Almanack*, earning him enough money to turn his focus to politics. He was elected to the Pennsylvania assembly in 1751 and served as its representative in Europe for many years. His scientific fame grew while he was abroad, earning him honorary degrees from St. Andrews and Oxford. He returned to America in 1775 to join the second Continental Congress and took an active role in the creation of Declaration of Independence, serving on the committee charged with preparing it. After 1776, he returned to Europe where he was instrumental in winning France's help during the Revolutionary War. He continued his diplomatic services until returning to America to help draft the U.S. Constitution. He later became the first U.S. postmaster general, established the first American circulating library, founded the American Philosophical Society for the Promotion of Useful Knowledge, and helped establish the University of Pennsylvania. Franklin died on April 17, 1790.

John Morton was born in Delaware in what was then known as Ridley, Pennsylvania, in 1724. He never knew his father, who died a few months before his birth, and was raised by his stepfather, who oversaw his education. He was a member of the Pennsylvania provincial assembly from 1755 to 1756, and then again from 1769 to 1775. Also in this period, he filled many posts in local politics, serving as justice of the peace, high sheriff, and presiding judge of the general court and the court of common pleas. He was elected to the first Continental Congress of 1774, and was reelected the following year. Along with Benjamin Franklin and James Wilson, he formed the majority of Pennsylvanian delegates that voted in favor of independence, a vote for which he received a large share of criticism from friends at the time. He was chairman of the committee that reported the Articles of Confederation. He died shortly after the report was presented, in April 1777.

James Wilson was born in St. Andrew's, Scotland, on September 14, 1742. In 1766, he immigrated to America to work at Philadelphia College, earning an honorary Master of Arts a few months later. He was admitted to the bar in 1767, after which he began his own practice in Reading, Pennsylvania, where he became involved with local politics. He joined the Continental Congress in 1775 and voted in favor of independence, joining with Benjamin Franklin and John Morton to form the majority for Pennsylvania. He lost favor in Pennsylvania shortly after when he criticized the new state constitution. He was recalled from Congress and was the victim of mob violence as a result. After the revolution, he became active in politics again, serving prominently on the Constitutional Convention of 1787. He was appointed to the Supreme Court in 1789, and his ruling in *Chisholm v. Georgia* led to the Eleventh Amendment to the Constitution. Unfortunately, his private life was led with much less order. After years of heavy speculation and gambling, the end of his life was plagued with creditors who hunted him, in his own words, "like a wild beast." Exhausted by his debts, he died on August 28, 1798.

Robert Morris was born in Lancashire, England, on January 20, 1734, moving to America at age thirteen. He apprenticed in the counting house of Charles Willing and entered into a very successful partnership with his son, Thomas Willing, after the elder Willing's death. He was elected to the Continental Congress in November 1775, where he served until 1778. During his term, he worked mostly to raise money for the continental army, loaning large sums of his own money and personally underwriting the privateers who ran the British blockades during the war. In 1781 his plan for a national bank was passed by Congress, leading to the creation of the Bank of North America. George Washington called him "the financier of the Revolution," and offered him the cabinet post of first secretary of the treasury, a job that Morris declined. He served in the Constitutional Convention of 1787 and took office as a senator from Pennsylvania from 1789 to 1795. His speculation in western lands destroyed his fortune and in 1798 he was arrested for debt. He spent three years in a debtor's prison. Morris's health and his finances never fully recovered, and he died in relative poverty on May 9, 1806.

George Taylor was born in Ireland in 1716. Very little is known about his early life before he immigrated to America in 1736 and found work at an iron furnace in Philadelphia. After the death of his employer, Taylor married the man's widow, becoming the owner and operator of the furnace. He was openly and outspokenly opposed to the British from 1763 onward, and took part in the provincial assembly of Philadelphia, 1764–69. He was elected to the Continental Congress in 1776, as one of the Pennsylvanian delegates sent to replace those who refused to vote in favor of independence. Although he did not take office in time to vote for independence, he did sign the declaration in August with the other delegates from Pennsylvania. He only served one term in the Continental Congress. In March 1777, he was elected to the new supreme executive council of Pennsylvania but he held the post for only a few weeks, giving up public office due to poor health. He died on February 23, 1781.

James Smith was born circa 1719 in Ireland. He received his education in Philadelphia, after which he studied law in the offices of his older brother, George, until he was admitted to the bar at age twenty-six. He set up his practice on the frontier of Cumberland County for four or five years, but could not find much legal work there and supported himself with surveying jobs before moving to York. Smith was known for his leadership in the struggle of the western counties against the eastern and for his strong stance against British policy. He was a member of a series of provincial conferences and congresses from 1774 to 1776 and in late July 1776 he was sent to Congress as a known supporter of independence. Smith retired from the Continental Congress in 1777, after which he held several local political posts. He was reelected to the Congress in 1785, but declined due to advancing age. He lived, however, for twenty-one more years, dying on July 11, 1806.

George Ross was born in New Castle, Delaware, on May 10, 1730, into a large family. His father, a clergyman, supervised the children's educations at home. When he was eighteen, he began to study law in the offices of his older brother in Philadelphia, but after he was admitted to the bar he opened his own practice in Lancaster. He first entered politics in 1768 when he was elected as a representative to the provincial assembly and continued to be reelected until 1776. He was sent to the Continental Congress in 1774, even though he was a Loyalist at the time. By 1775, he had turned to the Patriot side, and was an active member in the Pennsylvania Constitutional Convention of 1776. During that summer, he was one of the delegates sent to the Continental Congress to vote for independence. He withdrew from Congress in 1777 due to illness and afterwards served as a judge in the court of admiralty. He died in office on July 14, 1779.

George Clymer was born in Philadelphia on March 16, 1739. Orphaned when he was very young, Clymer was raised by a merchant uncle. He apprenticed in a counting room before striking out on his own, building a partnership known as Meredith & Clymer. He married the daughter of his partner, Reese Meredith, and it was in his father-in-law's house that he first met George Washington. Clymer became active in the local protests against the Tea Act and Stamp Act, and was elected to the Continental Congress in 1776; he continued to serve until 1780. Later, he was selected as a delegate to the Constitutional Convention of 1787, where he signed the U.S. Constitution. He was elected to the first session of U.S. Congress under the new Constitution but declined re-election, serving instead as Federal Indian Agent from 1781 to 1796. His last national public duty was a mission to the Cherokees in 1796. He continued to be active locally, serving as the first president of Philadelphia Bank, first president of the Philadelphia Academy of Fine Arts, and vice president of the Philadelphia Agricultural Society. He held all three posts until his death on January 23, 1813.

Benjamin Rush, the most famous American physician and medical teacher of his generation, was born on December 24, 1745, in Byberry, Pennsylvania. He received his undergraduate degree from the College of New Jersey, after which he earned his medical degree in Edinburgh, Scotland. In 1769, he was elected professor of chemistry in the college of Philadelphia, and took an active part in the local intellectual life. Politically, he joined the Sons of Liberty in 1773. He formed a close friendship with John Adams, and developed a strong friendship with Thomas Jefferson after his election to the Continental Congress in 1776. Rush served as surgeon general of the armies of the Middle Department in 1777, but resigned the position after less than a year. After a dispute with George Washington, Rush kept a low profile for the rest of the war, though he continued his medical practice, establishing the first American free dispensary in 1786. Adams appointed him treasurer of the U.S. Mint in 1797, and he held the post until his death on April 19, 1813.

DELAWARE

Caesar Rodney was born on October 7, 1728, in Dover, Delaware. He was taught informally by his father, who died when the younger Rodney was seventeen. In 1755, he was commissioned High Sheriff of Kent County, beginning his political career. After serving in several local assemblies, he was elected to the first Continental Congress in 1774. Rodney is best known for his dramatic arrival to vote for independence in the summer of 1776. After a trip to Sussex County to look into a threatened Loyalist uprising, he returned home to find word from fellow delegate Thomas McKean that the time had come to vote. He immediately rushed to Philadelphia. Since there were only three delegates from Delaware, one voting for and the other voting against, his vote gave Delaware the majority to vote in favor in independence. After leaving the Continental Congress, Rodney took a more active role in military life. He was appointed major general of militia by McKean, then acting as president of Delaware. In 1778, Rodney was himself elected president of Delaware, a post he held until 1781. He was a member of the Upper House of the state assembly from 1776 until his death on June 29, 1784.

George Read was born on his family's farm in Cecil County, Maryland, on September 18, 1733. He was admitted to the Philadelphia bar in 1753 and moved to New Castle, Delaware, to establish his practice the following year. He served in the local government as a member of the house of assembly of the Three Lower Counties for several years before joining the first Continental Congress in 1774. He was against the declaration at the time of the vote, but gave into the majority of the other Delaware delegates and signed it in August 1776. He was president of the committee that drafted the Delaware Constitution and served as governor of the state in 1777, when Governor John McKinly was captured by the British. Bad health kept him from taking an active role in politics for the rest of the Revolutionary War,

but he was a member of the Constitutional Convention of
1787 and served as senator from Delaware in the U.S.
Congress. He resigned the post in 1793 to become chief justice of Delaware, a position he held until his death on
September 21, 1798.

Thomas McKean was born in New London, Pennsylvania,
on March 19, 1734. He was educated at the New London
Academy, after which he studied law and was admitted to the
bar before he turned twenty-one. He was an elected delegate
to the first Continental Congress in 1774 and continued to
serve there almost without break until 1783. It was his summons that brought Caesar Rodney to the famous vote to carry
Delaware in favor of independence. He served on the committee to draw up the Articles of Confederation, was commissioned a colonel in the New Jersey militia, and served as
president of Delaware for a short time. He is credited along
with George Read with drafting the Delaware Constitution.
McKean's professional and political career is difficult to track
since he held office in two commonwealths at the same time.
In 1777, he was appointed chief justice of Pennsylvania, an
office he held for nearly twenty years. He was elected governor of Pennsylvania in 1799 and served three terms of three
years each. Even after his retirement in 1812, he remained locally active until his death on June 24, 1817.

MARYLAND

Charles Carroll was born on September 19, 1737, in
Annapolis, Maryland. He was educated by Jesuits in France
from age eight to seventeen, after which he studied law in
Paris and London. Despite his wealth, he suffered from discrimination as a Roman Catholic and was content to spend

most of his time out of the public eye after his return to America. He did not become involved in politics until 1773 when he argued against a series of articles defending the actions of the proprietary governor. In 1776, the Maryland Convention decided to support the movement for independence, and Carroll was elected on July 4 to represent Maryland in the Continental Congress. He served an important role in local Maryland politics, helping to frame the state Constitution, including in it a Declaration of Rights that forbade an established church for the state. He was elected to the state senate in 1781 and to the first U.S. Congress in 1788. He returned again to the state senate in 1790 and served there for ten years, retiring in 1800. Carroll was the last surviving signer of the Declaration of Independence and the richest man in the country when he died on November 14, 1832.

William Paca was born on October 31, 1740, in Abington, Maryland. His first education was at home, where he was tutored until he entered Philadelphia College at age fifteen. He graduated three years later with a master's degree, after which he read law in Annapolis. He moved to Europe for a time and continued his studies at the Inner Temple in England before applying for admission to the bar. His roots in law led him to take an active roll in politics after he returned to America, and he gained some local notoriety after he wrote articles against a poll tax originated by the royal governor. Paca was a local leader in the patriotic movement, serving in Maryland's state legislature in 1771 and joining the Continental Congress in 1774. He continued to serve in the Congress until 1779, when he left to accept appointment as chief justice of Maryland. He was elected governor in 1782 and served three one-year terms. Appointed federal district judge for the State of Maryland in

1789, Paca held that post until his death on October 23, 1799.

Samuel Chase was born in Abington, Somerset County, Maryland, on April 17, 1741. He studied law in Baltimore and began his practice in Annapolis, where he soon became involved in the local political struggles. He was aggressively anti-British and was an active and vocal member of the provincial assembly and later the Continental Congress, where he was elected in 1774. He was responsible for the provincial assembly's choice to favor independence; though his ride from Maryland to the Congress with fresh instructions for his state was not as dramatic as Caesar Rodney's, it was equally important. He remained in Congress until 1778, when he was accused of using inside information to deal in flour. Retiring in disgrace, he didn't become politically prominent again for a decade. Eventually he became chief judge of the general court of Maryland, and in 1796 President Washington appointed him an associate judge of the Supreme Court. He was known, and disliked, for his bullying tactics, particularly against Republicans, leading to his impeachment. Although he was acquitted, Chase was less aggressive afterwards, and continued to serve on the Supreme Court until his death on June 19, 1811.

Thomas Stone was born at Poynton Manor in Charles County, Maryland, in 1743, the grandson of the proprietary governor. He read law in Annapolis and after he was admitted to the bar in 1764, he set up his practice in Frederick. Stone was elected to the Continental Congress in 1775. Although he was more moderate than his fellow signers, he joined them in voting for independence. Stone served in Congress for several years, after which he served in the Maryland legislature, but was a reticent speaker in both jobs.

He was elected to attend the Constitutional Convention, but declined the office because of his wife's failing health. She died in 1787, and it is said that Stone never fully recovered from her death. He bought a ticket to travel to England, but died in Alexandria while waiting for the ship on October 5, 1787.

VIRGINIA

Richard Henry Lee was born to one of Virginia's most distinguished families on January 20, 1732, in Stratford, Westmoreland County, Virginia. He was educated in Europe, returning to Virginia in 1751, where he joined the local militia to fight in the French and Indian War. He was appointed justice of the peace in 1757 and was shortly after elected to the Virginia House of Burgesses, where he became prominently tied to the patriotic cause. In 1774, he was elected to attend the first Continental Congress, where he offered the Resolutions for Independence to the Congress in June 1776, leading to the creation of the Declaration of Independence. Lee continued to serve in the Constitutional Congress through the Revolutionary War, and was elected president of Congress in 1783. Following the establishment of the U.S. Constitution in 1787, he was elected to the first U.S. Senate, but retired in 1792 because of poor health. He died on June 19, 1794.

Thomas Jefferson was born in Albemarle County, Virginia, on April 13, 1743. He attended the College of William and Mary, after which he studied law. In 1769, he began serving in the House of Burgesses, and in 1775 was elected to the Continental Congress. Jefferson wrote the Declaration of Independence in 1776, but left Congress shortly after the signing. In 1779, he was elected governor of Virginia, serving one term before returning home to nurse his ailing wife who died the next year. In 1784, he was sent to France with Benjamin Franklin and John Adams; he stayed there until 1789, when he was appointed secretary of state under President Washington. Displeased with the government, he resigned in 1793 and formed the Democrat-Republican party, running for president in 1796. He lost to Adams and served as his vice president. He ran again in 1801 and won, serving two terms. Retiring from office in 1808, he spent the rest of his life in Monticello, establishing the University of Virginia, and carrying on a massive correspondence with old friends. Jefferson died on July 4, 1826, just a few hours before Adams, on the fiftieth anniversary of his Declaration of Independence.

Benjamin Harrison was born in Berkeley, Charles City County, Virginia, on April 5, 1726. He attended the College of William and Mary for a brief time, but returned home before receiving his degree when his father and two sisters were killed in a lightning strike. He was elected to the House of Burgesses in 1764, where he spoke out in his support of republican principles and stood up against the royal governor, even when he tried to bribe Harrison with an appointment to the executive council. He was elected to the Continental Congress in 1774 and was one of a party of representatives who met with General Washington in Cambridge, Massachusetts, to plan the future of the continental army. He returned to Virginia in 1777, where he rejoined the House of Burgesses and served as lieutenant in the local militia. Harrison was chosen as Speaker of the House in 1778 and elected governor of Virginia in 1782. He retired five years later and died on April 24, 1791, fifty years before his son, William Henry Harrison, became the ninth president of the United States.

George Wythe was born in Elizabeth County, Virginia, in 1726. He attended the College of William and Mary, after which he studied law and was made attorney general of Virginia in 1753. In 1754, Wythe was elected to the House of Burgesses, where he served until its dissolution. Secularly, he was elected to the Board of Visitors at the College of William and Mary in 1761; eight years later he became America's first professor of law. His students included Thomas Jefferson, Henry Clay, James Monroe, and John Marshal. Wythe was elected to the Continental Congress in 1775, where he served for two years until he was called back to Virginia in 1776 to help form the new government. He was elected Speaker of the Virginia House of Delegates in 1777 and was made one of the three chancellors of the State of Virginia in 1778. Unfailingly generous, Wythe planned to free his slaves in his will, giving them a portion of the family property. Upon learning of this, his grandnephew and chief beneficiary, George Wythe Sweeny, decided to enlarge his own share of the estate by poisoning his great uncle's slaves, but also killed Wythe by accident. He died on June 8, 1806.

Francis Lightfoot Lee was born in Westmoreland, Virginia, on October 14, 1734, two years after his brother Richard Henry Lee. He was educated at home and became active in public life in 1765 when he was elected to the House of Burgesses. He continued to serve there for many years. Lee was a noted radical, siding with Patrick Henry against the Stamp Act. He was not initially elected to the Continental Congress, but was sent there when another delegate, Richard Bland, asked to be relieved of office. Though he was over-shadowed in the Congress by his more outspoken brother, he was firmly in favor of independence and was known as an ardent patriot. Lee arrived in time to vote for independence, and continued to energetically serve on several committees in

Congress, although he usually stayed silent in debates. He died on January 11, 1797.

Carter Braxton was born to a wealthy family on Newington Plantation in King and Queen County, Virginia, on September 10, 1736. He attended the College of William and Mary and married young. After the death of his wife only two years after their marriage, he spent several years in England, returning to America in 1760 when he was elected to the House of Burgesses. Braxton sided with Patrick Henry and others in opposition to the Stamp Act and joined the Committee of Public Safety after the House of Burgesses was dissolved in 1774. He was appointed to the Continental Congress in 1775, after the death of a Virginia delegate, and took his seat in February 1776. During the war, Braxton invested heavily in shipping and privateering against the British and as a result lost most of his wealth through shipping losses. His finances never fully recovered and he was forced to leave his inherited country estate for simpler quarters in Richmond near the end of his life. He died on October 10, 1797.

Thomas Nelson Jr. was born into a family of influential merchants and planters in Yorktown, Virginia, on December 26, 1738. He received his degree from Cambridge University, returning to Virginia in 1761, when he became well acquainted with Thomas Jefferson during the latter's student years. Elected to the House of Burgesses in 1774, he served there until it was dissolved. Afterwards, he joined the Virginia provincial convention and created the Virginia militia, assuming the role of commander. He joined the Continental Congress in May 1776, where he shared the resolutions of the Virginia convention, sparking Richard Henry Lee's declaration and the Declaration of Independence. Nelson served in the Continental Congress until poor health led him to retire in 1777, after which he rejoined the militia as brigadier general. In 1781, he was elected governor of Virginia and served as both civil governor and commander in chief of the Virginia militia, which thrived under him, and was used by both the continental army and French forces during the Siege of Yorktown in the autumn of 1781. Illness forced him to retire that October, and he settled into a small estate in Hanover County with his family. Nelson died on January 4, 1789.

NORTH CAROLINA

Joseph Hewes was born in Kingston, New Jersey, on January 23, 1730. He attended Princeton College, after which he established a shipping business in Wilmington, North Carolina. By the time of the revolution, he had amassed a fortune. He was elected to the colonial assembly in 1766; he continued to serve until it was dissolved by the royal governor, after which he was sent to the Continental Congress. Hewes was most noted for his work on the marine committee, where he practically served as the first head of the United States Navy. He fell ill in 1779 and died later that year, on November 10, 1779.

John Penn was born near Port Royal, Virginia, on May 17, 1741. Though his education was informal at best, access to the library of Edmund Pendleton, a well-respected lawyer in the area and Penn's relative, allowed him to educate himself. By the time he was twenty-two, he had been admitted to the Virginia bar. He moved to Williamsboro in Granville County, North Carolina, in 1774, and set up a law practice, establishing himself professionally and politically. He was quickly accepted into the political community and was elected to both the provincial Congress and the Continental Congress in 1775. He served in the Continental Congress from 1775 to 1777 and then again from 1778 to 1780, at which point he was appointed to the board of war. Penn retired almost completely from public life after 1781 due to poor health. In his retirement, he focused mostly on his law practice. He died on September 14, 1788.

William Hooper was born in Boston on June 28, 1742. He graduated from Harvard College in 1760, after which he studied law under James Otis, a well-known advocate for colonial rights. He settled in Wilmington, North Carolina, in 1767, where he opened his own practice. He was not particularly popular in the area; he had sided against the frontiersmen Regulators in the western Carolinas and there was still a great deal of residual resentment in the years that followed. But he was respected enough to be elected to the Continental Congress in 1774, where he continued until 1776. After returning to North Carolina, Hooper served in the state legislature for five years. When the British captured Wilmington, his property was nearly destroyed, forcing him to move to Hillsboro. In 1789 he was appointed to the federal bench, but retired a year later due to failing health. He died on October 14, 1790.

SOUTH CAROLINA

Arthur Middleton was born near Charleston, South Carolina, on June 26, 1742. His father, Henry Middleton, owned a score of plantations and close to eight hundred slaves. As the oldest son, Middleton was given a very expensive education in England, graduating from Cambridge in

1773 and reading law at the Middle Temple. In spite of his British education, he was a staunch patriot, serving on the Council of Safety in Charleston in 1775 and then in the Continental Congress in 1776. As an officer in the militia, he was captured by the British when Charleston was overrun in 1781 and held prisoner for several months, along with his fellow signers Thomas Heyward Jr. and Edward Rutledge. Although most of his fortune was destroyed during the Revolutionary War, he remained actively engaged in politics until his death on January 1, 1787.

Thomas Heyward Jr. was born on his father's plantation in St. Helena's (later St. Luke's) Parish, South Carolina, on July 28, 1746, into a wealthy, established family. His early education was handled mostly at home, after which he went to England to read law at the Middle Temple. Heyward was in England during the early stages of the revolution, but became involved in politics almost immediately after his return to America. He soon drew attention as an active patriot and was elected to the Continental Congress in 1775. He stayed there until 1778, when he returned to South Carolina to serve as a circuit judge. After the fall of Charleston, he was taken prisoner by the British along with fellow signers Arthur Middleton and Edward Rutledge and was held with them at a prison in St. Augustine, Florida, for several months. Heyward resumed his judgeship following the war, but retired to focus on his plantation when he was forty-three. He died on March 6, 1809.

Edward Rutledge was born in Charleston, South Carolina, on November 23, 1749. Educated in law at Oxford, he served for some time on the English bar before returning to America early in 1773. Rutledge, along with his brother John, was elected to the first session of the Continental

Congress in 1774, but when elections were held for the second session, John chose to return home, where he became engaged in local politics, while Edward stayed with the Congress. After signing the Declaration of Independence, Rutledge left Congress to return to South Carolina and join the local militia, where he served as an officer and attained the rank of captain. Although he was reelected to the Continental Congress, he chose to stay in Charleston and was captured by the British when the city fell. He was active in the local legislature and state conventions after the war and was elected governor in 1798, but his health faded rapidly and he was barely able to complete his term of office. He died on January 1, 1800.

Thomas Lynch Jr. was born in Winyah, South Carolina, on August 5, 1749. He was educated in England, first at Eton and Cambridge, from which he graduated with honors, and afterwards he read law in the Middle Temple. Lynch, though, did not care for law and chose instead to work as a planter, returning home in 1772. Through his father's influence, he was elected to public office at a very early age, and was commissioned a company commander in the South Carolina regiment by 1775. He was elected to the Continental Congress to support or replace his father, who was suffering from a recent stroke. Lynch's own health was weak after an attack of bilious fever, and he returned to South Carolina only a few months after signing the Declaration of Independence. His father's death on the way home weakened him further, and he and his wife planned a trip away in late 1776 to recuperate. They boarded a boat to the West Indies, intending to sail from there to southern France, but the ship disappeared and the Lynches were presumed lost at sea.

GEORGIA

Lyman Hall was born in Wallingford, Connecticut, on April 12, 1724. He graduated from Yale in 1756 and spent a few years working as a minister before training as a physician. He bought land in Georgia in 1760 and helped establish the community of Sunbury, where he set up a plantation and continued to practice medicine. His parish elected him delegate to the Continental Congress in spring 1775, where he was involved in provisioning food and medicine for the colonial army. Hall was annually reelected to the Continental Congress, bringing his family north with him in 1778 when the British destroyed his home and plantation. After the war, he moved to Savannah, where he continued to practice medicine and was elected governor of Georgia in 1783. During his term of office, he recommended the setting aside of a grant of land for the support of a college, leading to the development of Franklin College and the University of Georgia. Later he served a single one-year term as governor, an additional year in the assembly, and then one year as a judge. He retired to private life after that and died on October 19, 1790.

Button Gwinnett was born in England at Down Hatherley, Gloucestershire, circa 1735. Little is known about his early life before 1765, when he was living in Charleston, South Carolina, and working as a merchant. That year, he managed to acquire a large tract of land in Georgia, where he and his wife moved shortly afterwards. He quickly became involved in local politics and was elected as a delegate to the Continental Congress in 1776. He voted for and signed the Declaration of Independence before returning to Georgia late in the summer. Gwinnett served notably in that state's legislature, where he is credited with drafting the constitution for the new state. He butted heads with military authorities, especially Brigadier General Lachlan McIntosh, over his failed attempt to invade Florida in order to secure Georgia's southern border. McIntosh challenged Gwinnett, calling him a scoundrel and a liar, leading to a duel outside of Savannah on May 16, 1777. Both were wounded, but McIntosh survived while Gwinnett died three days later, on May 19, 1777.

George Walton was born in Prince Edward County near Farmville, Virginia, in 1741. He taught himself law after moving to Savannah in 1769, and was admitted to the bar in 1774. Walton became actively involved in local politics following the Boston Tea Party and was elected to the Continental Congress in 1776. He served as colonel of the militia in the siege of Savannah in 1778, during which he was wounded, captured, and then exchanged. He was then elected governor of Georgia in 1779, a post he held for only two months. He returned to the Continental Congress in 1780 and served another year, working on several committees, most notably negotiating treaties with the Iroquois and Cherokee Indians. In Georgia, he held the post of chief justice during the confederation period, and was elected governor again in 1789. In 1795 he was sent to fill an unexpired term in the U.S. Senate, to which he was not reelected. He spent his final years in retirement, living in Augusta and helping with the formation of the University of Georgia. He died on February 2, 1804.

ALSO NOTABLE

George Washington was born on February 22, 1732, in Westmoreland County, Virginia. At age fifteen, he began working as an assistant surveyor, eventually earning appointment as official surveyor of Culpeper County. Commissioned a lieutenant colonel in 1754, he fought in the French and Indian War, after which he returned to Virginia, concentrating on managing his lands and serving in the Virginia House of Burgesses. He became active in the patriotic cause after the House of Burgesses was dissolved, and was elected to the Continental Congress in 1774. Once he was elected commander in chief of the continental army in 1775, he was unavoidingly absent from the Congress most of the time, preventing him from signing the Declaration of Independence. He led the continental army to victory in 1781, and when the new nation struggled under the Articles of Confederation, he started the movement for the Constitutional Convention of 1787. After the U.S. Constitution was ratified, Washington was unanimously elected the first president of the United States. He served two terms before retiring to his estate in Mount Vernon, near Alexandria, Virginia, where he died less than three years later of a throat infection, on December 14, 1799.

IN CONGRESS, JULY 4, 1776.

The unanimous Declaration of the thirteen united States of America.

The Declaration of Independence
July 4, 1776

WHEN IN THE course of human events, it becomes necessary for one people to dissolve the political bands which have connected them with another, and to assume among the powers of the earth, the separate and equal station to which the laws of nature and of nature's God entitle them, a decent respect to the opinions of mankind requires that they should declare the causes which impel them to the separation.

We hold these truths to be self-evident, that all men are created equal, that they are endowed by their Creator with certain unalienable rights; that among these are life, liberty and the pursuit of happiness. That to secure these rights, governments are instituted among men, deriving their just powers from the consent of the governed, that whenever any form of government becomes destructive of these ends, it is the right of the people to alter or to abolish it, and to institute new government, laying its foundation on such principles and organizing its powers in such form, as to them shall seem most likely to effect their safety and happiness. Prudence, indeed, will dictate that governments long established should not be changed for light and transient causes; and accordingly all experience hath shown, that mankind are more disposed to suffer, while evils are sufferable, than to right themselves by abolishing the forms to which they are accustomed. But when a long train of abuses and usurpations, pursuing invariably the same object evinces a design to reduce them under absolute despotism, it is their right, it is their duty, to throw off such government, and to provide new guards for their future security. Such has been the patient sufferance of these colonies; and such is now the necessity which constrains them to alter their former systems of government. The history of the present King of Great Britain is a history of repeated injuries and usurpations, all having in direct object the establishment of an absolute tyranny over these States. To prove this, let facts be submitted to a candid world.

He has refused his assent to laws, the most wholesome and necessary for the public good.

He has forbidden his governors to pass laws of immediate and pressing importance, unless suspended in their operation till his assent should be obtained; and when so suspended, he has utterly neglected to attend to them.

He has refused to pass other laws for the accommodation of large districts of people, unless those people would relinquish the right of representation in the legislature, a right inestimable to them and formidable to tyrants only.

He has called together legislative bodies at places unusual, uncomfortable, and distant from the depository or their public records, for the sole purpose of fatiguing them into compliance with his measures.

He has dissolved representative houses repeatedly, for opposing with manly firmness his invasions on the rights of the people.

He has refused for a long time, after such dissolutions, to cause others to be elected; whereby the legislative powers, incapable of annihilation, have returned to the people at large for their exercise; the state remaining in the mean time exposed to all the dangers of invasion from without, and convulsions within.

He has endeavored to prevent the population of these states; for that purpose obstructing the laws for naturalization of foreigners; refusing to pass others to encourage their migration hither, and raising the conditions of new appropriations of lands.

He has obstructed the administration of justice, by refusing his assent to laws for establishing judiciary powers.

He has made judges dependent on his will alone, for the tenure of their offices, and the amount and payment of their salaries.

He has erected a multitude of new offices, and sent hither swarms of officers to harass our people, and eat out their substance.

He has kept among us, in times of peace, standing armies, without the consent of our legislatures.

He has affected to render the military independent of and superior to the civil power.

He has combined with others to subject us to a jurisdiction foreign to our constitution, and unacknowledged by our laws; giving his assent to their acts of pretended legislation:

For quartering large bodies of armed troops among us:

For protecting them, by a mock trial, from punishment for any murders which they should commit on the inhabitants of these states:

For cutting off our trade with all parts of the world:

For imposing taxes on us without our consent:

For depriving us in many cases, of the benefits of trial by jury:

For transporting us beyond seas to be tried for pretended offenses:

For abolishing the free system of English laws in a neighboring province, establishing therein an arbitrary government, and enlarging its boundaries so as to render it at once an example and fit instrument for introducing the same absolute rule into these colonies:

For taking away our charters, abolishing our most valuable laws, and altering fundamentally the forms of our governments:

For suspending our own legislatures, and declaring themselves invested with power to legislate for us in all cases whatsoever.

He has abdicated government here, by declaring us out of his protection and waging war against us.

He has plundered our seas, ravaged our coasts, burnt our towns, and destroyed the lives of our people.

He is at this time transporting large armies of foreign mercenaries to complete the works of death, desolation and tyranny, already begun with circumstances of cruelty and perfidy scarcely paralleled in the most barbarous ages, and totally unworthy the head of a civilized nation.

He has constrained our fellow citizens taken captive on the high seas to bear arms against their country, to become the executioners of their friends and brethren, or to fall themselves by their hands.

He has excited domestic insurrections amongst us, and has endeavored to bring on the inhabitants of our frontiers, the merciless Indian savages, whose known rule of warfare is an undistinguished destruction of all ages, sexes and conditions.

In every state of these oppressions we have petitioned for redress in the most humble terms; our repeated petitions have been answered only by repeated injury. A prince, whose character is thus marked by every act which may define a tyrant, is unfit to be the ruler of a free people.

Nor have we been wanting in attentions to our British brethren. We have warned them from time to time of attempts by their legislature to extend an unwarrantable jurisdiction over us. We have reminded them of the circumstances of our emigration and settlement here. We have appealed to their native justice and magnanimity, and we have conjured them by the ties of our common kindred to disavow these usurpations, which would inevitably interrupt our connections and correspondence. They too have been deaf to the voice of justice and of consanguinity. We must, therefore, acquiesce in the necessity, which denounces our separation, and hold them, as we hold the rest of mankind, enemies in war, in peace friends.

We, therefore, the representatives of the United States of America, in General Congress, assembled, appealing to the Supreme Judge of the world for the rectitude of our intentions, do, in the name, and by authority of the good people of these colonies, solemnly publish and declare, that these United Colonies are, and of right ought to be free and independent States; that they are absolved from all allegiance to the British Crown, and that all political connection between them and the state of Great Britain, is and ought to be totally dissolved; and that as free and independent states, they have full power to levy war, conclude peace, contract alliances, establish commerce, and to do all other acts and things which independent states may of right do. And for the support of this declaration, with a firm reliance on the protection of Divine Providence, we mutually pledge to each other our lives, our fortunes and our sacred honor.

❧ The Star-Spangled Banner ❧
by Francis Scott Key

O say, can you see, by the dawn's early light,
What so proudly we hail'd at the twilight's last gleaming?
Whose broad stripes and bright stars, thro' the perilous fight,
O'er the ramparts we watch'd, were so gallantly streaming?
And the rockets' red glare, the bombs bursting in air,
Gave proof thro' the night that our flag was still there.
O say, does that star-spangled banner yet wave
O'er the land of the free and the home of the brave?

On the shore dimly seen thro' the mists of the deep,
Where the foe's haughty host in dread silence reposes,
What is that which the breeze, o'er the towering steep,
As it fitfully blows, half conceals, half discloses?
Now it catches the gleam of the morning's first beam,
In full glory reflected, now shines on the stream:
'Tis the star-spangled banner: O, long may it wave
O'er the land of the free and the home of the brave!

And where is that band who so vauntingly swore
That the havoc of war and the battle's confusion,
A home and a country should leave us no more?
Their blood has wash'd out their foul footsteps' pollution.
No refuge could save the hireling and slave
From the terror of flight or the gloom of the grave:

And the star-spangled banner in triumph doth wave
O'er the land of the free and the home of the brave.

O thus be it ever when free-men shall stand
Between their lov'd home and the war's desolation;
Blest with vict'ry and peace, may the heav'n-rescued land
Praise the Pow'r that hath made and preserv'd us a nation!
Then conquer we must, when our cause it is just,
And this be our motto: "In God is our trust!"
And the star-spangled banner in triumph shall wave
O'er the land of the free and the home of the brave!